Simple
Sermons
on
Simple
Themes

Simple Sermons on Simple Themes

W. Herschel Ford

BAKER BOOK HOUSE
Grand Rapids, Michigan 49516

Copyright 1941, 1957 by Zondervan Publishing House
Grand Rapids, Michigan

Reprinted 1988 by Baker Book House
Grand Rapids, Michigan
with the permission of the copyright holder

ISBN: 0-8010-3543-0

Printed in the United States of America

INTRODUCTION

It gives me pleasure to introduce, with a strong word of approval and gratitude, this volume of sermons by my son in the ministry. I remember distinctly when he made complete committal to the Savior's will in answering the call to preach. I have followed him through his college and seminary days and into his pastorates.

I find great delight in the clearness, accuracy, simplicity, pungency and hearty and direct appeal of these messages which he has delivered from the pulpit.

The author is a soul winner, a gospel preacher of strength and power, and these dynamic messages on a number of vital gospel themes to the saved and to the lost proclaim clearly the gospel and constitute the earnest appeal of a loving, hot-hearted preacher. More and more the preachers ought to stay in the close relationship of the gospel of Jesus Christ in their proclamation of the New Testament message to a lost, suffering world, and these messages make a fine illustration of this growing, universal demand on the part of the ministers of the gospel.

I could wish that many preachers and other Christians may have the benefit of these ringing messages and that they may find response in the souls of many lost ones.

L. R. SCARBOROUGH, *President*
Southwestern Baptist Theological Seminary

Contents

Contents

. . . in simplicity and godly sincerity, not with fleshly wisdom, but by the grace of God, we have had our conversation in the world . . .

—II CORINTHIANS 1:12

been thrown into the pit, and soldiers have covered his body with stones. What is the epitaph that I read there? It is not carved upon stone, but as I listen I hear it sobbing on the breeze: "O my son, Absalom, my son, my son Absalom! Would God I had died for thee, O Absalom, my son, my son!" The one who is sobbing is David, the mighty King. The one who is dead is Absalom, his handsome son. And these sad words are the epitaph over the tomb.

Why is Absalom here? Why has the pit been digged? Why these stones? Why this sobbing of the king? Let us look into this story and learn a lesson for our own hearts.

I. The Story of Absalom

David was the great king of Israel. He ruled during the golden age of his country. He had wealth, honor, fame and a fine family. His third son was Absalom. He loved him with all his heart. You would think that this son would have grown to be an honor to his father, for he had everything in his favor, but his heart was black with sin. He was jealous of his own father and wanted the throne. He used all his charm and personality to win people to his side. He had plenty of charm, for we read that there was not a man in Israel as handsome as he was, and that he had not a single blemish on his body from the crown of his head to the soles of his feet.

Day after day Absalom stood at the gates of the city, and there he met the people who came up to make their complaints and to present their grievances.

He would say to them, "Your cause is just, but there is no one to hear you. If I were the judge of this land you would have justice." A man would come up to kneel to him since he was the king's son, but he would grasp the man by the shoulders and pull him up and say, "No, you must not bow before me, I am your friend," and then he would put his arms around the man and kiss him and express again his friendship for him. No wonder we read that he "stole the hearts of the men of Israel."

Soon he had gathered a great army about him and was leading a rebellion against the king. The time of the battle comes and David is going forth to fight, but his men said to him, "No, you must not go, you are worth ten thousand men." Then David replied, "I will stay behind if you will grant me just one request — deal gently with Absalom for my sake."

David's army was victorious, and while Absalom was fleeing, his long beautiful hair became entangled in the low-hanging bows of the tree and Joab came along and killed him. A messenger ran back to give David the news, but David did not ask about the battle—he cried out, "Is my son Absalom safe?" The messenger said, "No, the young man is dead." Then we see the old king as he drags himself up to his room above the wall. This is one of the most dramatic scenes in the Bible. As David climbs the stairs I hear that cry wrung from his lips, "O my son Absalom, my son, my son Absalom! Would God I had died for thee, O Absalom, my son, my son!"

II. The Sorrow of the Father's Heart

David had many sons. Why did he grieve over the loss of one? You see a father who has ten sons, and when one of them dies you say to the father, "Why do you weep? You have many sons left." But that will not comfort him, for a father's heart is not like that. He loves all of his children, and the loss of one breaks his heart. Sometime ago I read an old poem that told a touching story. A rich man had no children, but a poor man who lived near him had seven children, and found it very difficult to make a living for them. One day the rich man wrote a letter to the poor man saying, "Give me one of your children and I will give you a house and land and money." The father read the letter to the mother that night and they decided that this would be the best course. They went into the bedroom to choose the child who would be given away. When they came to the first bed the mother said, "Oh, he is just a baby. I can't give him up." In the next bed was a little boy with tear stains upon his cheek. He had cried himself to sleep. The father said, "We must keep him." In the next bed was a little child who had suffered greatly. The mother said, "We cannot let him go. We must keep him and care for him." In the next bed was a little boy with a smile upon his face. He was always happy and brought joy and laughter into the home. They couldn't possibly give him up. Then they came to the little girl who looked so very much like her mother, and the father, who loved her devotedly, said, "No, we must keep her." They passed on into the room of the eldest son. He was steady and trustworthy, and they felt that they could not do without him. Then they came to the last bed, and there lay the wayward son. He was the one who had gone astray and had caused them so much trouble, but the mother said, "We cannot let him go. He would have no mother there to pray for him." And so the father sat down and wrote a letter and told the rich man that they could not give up one of their children, and in his heart he was just deciding that he would work a little harder in order to care for them all.

Is there a loving father anywhere who is willing to give up one of his children? No, of course not. As we think of our children we say, "I could not part with one of them." What a sorrowful thing it was then that David had to give up his son, even though that son had rebelled against him.

Some explorers of an Egyptian tomb found the burial place of a little child. For three thousand years the tomb had been sealed, but carved above the niche were the words, "Oh, my life, my love, my little one! I would God I had died in thy stead." The explorers took off their hats, sealed the tomb back up and left love to its eternal vigil.

When Calvin Coolidge was in the White House, one of his sons died, and Mr. Coolidge sorrowfully said, "He took the glory of the presidency away with him."

Some day you may lose your boy or girl. I would like to ask you two questions. First, could you stand it? Do you have a Saviour to comfort you and carry

you through such an hour? Second, have you taught
that child the way of God, and is he ready to live
and die and face the judgment? You daddies and
mothers must not give all of your time to the world.
There must be some time for God, and for leading
your child in the way everlasting.

III. Retribution of a Past Sin

David was "a man after God's own heart," but
there came a day when God's man grievously sinned
and God said, "the sword shall not depart from thy
house." As David wept over Absalom that day, he
knew that he was paying part of the price of his
sin. As he climbed up the stairs he was forced to
say to himself, "It is my own fault. I brought this
upon myself because of my sin." Since that time many
fathers have seen their sons go off into sin and they,
too, have had to say, "It is all my fault. It came because of my own sin." A certain boy was arrested
because of a crime that he had committed. The
preacher in the community went to see the mother and
tried to comfort her, but she would only say, "It is
all my fault. There was a time when I prayed for
my boy every day. I took him to church and tried
to lead him in the right way, but after a while I
forgot to pray. I neglected my church and my Christian duty and my boy drifted off into sin. It is not
his fault altogether — it is mine." That is true of
so many parents. God has given these children to
us. Oh, let us lead them to Him.

James Stirling was a temperance lecturer in Scotland. At sixty years of age he was a drunkard, but he was saved by the grace of God and made over into a good and sober man. For the next twenty years he worked for the cause of temperance, but his son became a drunkard, and finally committed suicide. The cry of this broken hearted father was like the cry of David as he said, "If I had been a sober man all my life, this might not have happened." Yes, you love your son, and would do nothing to harm him. Do you want to help him? Then live a good life and set the right example before him and lead him in Christ's way. If you do not lead that child in the right way some day he will go out to break your heart and you will say, "I would God that I had led my child rightly and set the right example before him."

I call upon you fathers to give your hearts to the Lord and to line up in His church. Make pals of your boys. Do not send them to church; come with them. Pray for them. So live that you can say, "If my boy goes wrong it will not be my fault."

IV. WE SEE NEXT THE TRAGEDY OF A WASTED LIFE

Absalom had wonderful opportunities. He had wealth, position, training and personality. He could have been a great king, but he was a miserable failure. He wasted his life.

Suppose you saw a man in a boat, holding in his hand a bag of gold and throwing it out into the ocean. You would cry out to him, "Quit wasting that gold." Life is more important than money. God has given you just one life. It will be very short at the best. I would say to you, "Young man, quit wasting your life! Use it for God and for others."

Absalom built a costly tomb. He expected to occupy it when he died. He expected to have a great state funeral with all the nations to mourn, and with the grand people of his time marching by in royal robes. He expected the coming generations to pass by his tomb and say, "Here lies Absalom, the mighty king." But how different it was. Instead of resting in a marble mausoleum, his body, which once was so handsome and flawless, was broken and thrown into a pit. He was covered with stones, and there was no one to mourn him except the poor broken-hearted father. Many a young man starts out in life with wonderful possibilities and prospects, but because of lack of reverence or lack of purity and lack of faith in God, he comes to a miserable end. Instead of leaving a great monument, all that is left is some broken hearted father or mother crying out, "My son, my son."

A young man was found drowned in one of our rivers. The officers were not able to identify his body, and an account of the tragedy was published in the newspapers. In a few days time two hundred letters came from two hundred fathers and mothers, asking for a description of the boy. What a terrible fact was revealed—a fact of wayward, wasted lives and broken hearted parents.

Two young men were taking a journey on a train. At the end of the first day one of them went to the wash-room to clean up and to change his linen. The other one said, "Are you nearing the end of your journey?" The first man replied, "No, I have another day yet to go." "Why then," said the other, "did you clean up and change your linen?" He replied, "I find that the best way to get to the end of the way clean is to keep clean as I go along." Young men, if you want to come to the end of the way clean, start out in the right way. Live a good life and stay clean every day. Don't waste your life, give it over to Christ and use it in the wisest and best service in the world.

V. A Picture of God's Heart

David wept and said, "Would God that I had died in thy stead." No human father can do that, but Christ felt that way about the world, and did something about it. He wept over a sinful world, but that was not all—He went out to die for it and said, "Though you have sinned, I will take your place and bear all your sins and cleanse you and take you to Heaven." David wept over Absalom, but it was too late. God is weeping over you, but it is not too late. He will save you now if you will come to Him.

Absalom was a wicked, wayward son, but his father loved him, and though you, too, are evil and sinful, God loves you. He loves you far more than David could love his son. He loves you with all His heart, and wants you to have hope and heaven, and all the best things of time and eternity.

Dr. S. D. Gordon tells of two brothers, Tom and Joe, who lived with their father upon a farm. Tom was quite careless and one day left the bars of the pasture fence down. The cows wandered out into the field where they devoured much of the crop. The father told him that if this happened again he would be forced to punish him severely. Everything went along all right for a few weeks, and then Tom was careless again. Once more the cows went into the field and destroyed more of the crop. The father took Tom out to punish him, but Joe, the elder brother, interceded. He stood before the father and said, "Father do you remember reading the fifty-third chapter of Isaiah at breakfast this morning?" "Yes," said the father, "it is a wonderful chapter." Then Joe said, "That chapter told about how One suffered for another and I want to suffer for Tom — let me take his punishment." And then the tears came into the father's eyes. He put his arms around both of the boys and the three of them wept together. There was no punishment for Tom that day and never again did he forget, never again did he disobey.

Oh, my friends, that is what Jesus did for us. We had sinned and the great Father had reserved his punishment for us, but Jesus came and not only offered Himself, but actually took our sins in His own body and died upon the cross for us.

God help every father and mother to say, "I will give my heart to Christ and will live for Him. I will set the right example before my children." May God help every son to say, "I, too, will give my heart to Christ. I will live for Him so that my father will never be forced to weep and to cry out, 'My son, my son.'"

3

LOOKING UP TO GOD

I will lift up mine eyes unto the hills, from whence cometh my help.—PSALM 121:1

THE DIFFERENCE in men is the difference in vision. One man is a stone mason and another man is a famous sculptor. They both work with the same material, but one has vision and the other has none. One man is a house painter and the other is a talented artist. They both work with the same materials, but one has vision and the other has not. The Bible says, "Where there is no vision the people perish." Napoleon said, "The world was made by men of vision."

Isaiah said, "I saw the Lord high and lifted up." That vision changed his entire life. Daniel opened his windows toward the holy city and that vision changed all of life for him. Peter said, "We were the eye witnesses of his majesty." It was that vision which transformed the life of the early believers. A man who has never had a vision of God is of the earth earthy. He looks down upon material things; he never rises to the heights. He never looks up to God.

Behold the sunflower of the field. Whatever winds

36

may blow, this flower always turns its face toward
its God, the sun. That is what we need to do—in
all the changing circumstances of life, we are to look
up to our great God.

The Psalmist who wrote the hundred twenty-first
Psalm was a real human being. He had had many
experiences and had suffered much. He knew what
the grip of the world was. Out of his large experience
he wrote, "I have seen many things, I have had con-
tact with many people, I have suffered many things,
but after all I have learned that the remedy for every
ill is found in looking up to God." Let us learn a
lesson today as we "Lift up our eyes unto the hills."

I. We Are to Look Up for Cleansing from Sin

"All have sinned and come short of the glory of
God." We need cleansing. Where can the weary soul
find this cleansing? We find it in one place only—
the burdened soul must look up to Jesus. You can
find all sorts of men in the world, but you can never
find a perfect one. You see some man who lives a
beautiful, useful life, and you say, "Surely this man
is without sin," but deep down in his nature there
is the germ of sin, and some day it will crop out.
All of us have committed sin and all of us need a
cleansing.

A party of people were going down into a coal
mine, one lady wearing a white dress. Her friends
told her that she ought not to wear this dress. She
appealed to the guide, and said, "Can't I wear this

white dress?" He said, "There is nothing to prevent you from wearing a white dress down into the mine, but there is much to prevent your wearing a white dress out of the mine." And so if we go out into this old world we find that our garments are soon being stained with the blackness of sin. There is one place for cleansing, and that is in His blood.

Bruce, the king of Scotland, fled before his enemies. He left his castle and plunged deep into the forest. Soon he heard the baying of his own blood-hounds, for his enemies had come to the castle and had sent them out upon his trail. He knew that they would soon find him, but soon he found a little stream, and plunging in he walked down-stream for several miles before emerging on the other side. The trail was lost to the blood hounds and the king was safe. And so it is with us. We try to evade our sins, but they come baying at our heels. Is there no release from them? Yes, "There is a fountain filled with blood, drawn from Immanuel's veins, and sinners plunged beneath that flood lose all their guilty stains."

Do you have sin in your life? Then look up to Jesus. He alone can cleanse your heart and save you and make you free.

II. We Are to Look Up for Guidance in Life's Choices

Life is full of choices. Every day we stand at the parting of the ways and ask the question, "Which way shall I take?" In our strength we can find no

answer, no guide. We need one to whisper to our
hearts, and to say, "Here is the way, walk ye in
it."

How can we find that guidance in Him? It is
found through surrender and prayer. If we give ourselves fully to Him and pray for His guidance He
will give it to us. "In all thy ways acknowledge
Him, and He will direct thy paths."

If you are choosing a career you ought to pray
about it. The Christian is not only to make a living—
he must make a life. He must not only make good—
he must be of service. There are manys ways open
to the young person as he begins life. Ask God to
guide you into that best place.

Are you choosing a life mate? Do you want to
marry and have a home and children? Somewhere
in the world there is one whom God wants you to
have, the one who was made for you. You ought
to pray for God to guide you to each other. Too
many unions are ruined because young people rush
into marriage. Marriage is a spiritual thing, and if
it is not approached from a spiritual standpoint it
is likely to end in a wreck.

Every day we are making smaller choices. The
old preachers used to pray for God "to choose our
changes." Each morning we should ask God to help
us make the right choices for that day. There are
two roads of life. One is the right way and the other
is the wrong. One leads upward and the other leads
downward. One ends in heaven—the other in hell.
One is the way of usefulness, and the other is the way

of worthlessness. God help us to look up and to make the right choices.

III. WE ARE TO LOOK UP FOR HELP WHEN WE ARE TEMPTED

When temptations flow over the soul we are prone to say, "Certainly no one was ever tempted as I am." Yes, there was One. He came into the world and took upon Himself the form of a man and all the temptations that can ever come to us crowded in upon Him, but He had remembered to look up and God gave Him strength to overcome. We read, "He was in all points tempted like as we are, yet without sin." Again we read, "God will not allow you to be tempted above that you are able to bear, but will with the temptation provide a way of escape." We read again, "He has suffered being tempted, and He is able to help them that are tempted." Our trouble is that we do not look up. We look North and South and East and West. We look about us, but we fail to look up. God has help for those who are sorely tried, but it is only in looking up to Him that we receive this help and strength.

The Bible says, "resist the devil and he will flee from you." Temptations came to David and he forgot God and embraced the sin. He failed to look up. There is a devil and if we try to resist him he will put up a fight, but we can conquer if we look up and enlist God on our side.

A Chinese man was a slave to the opium habit for thirty-nine years. This is a deep-seated habit, and

one from which few men escape. But this man found
Christ and overcame the bad habit. When someone
asked him how he had done this he simply replied,
"On my two knees." Yes, we can see God clearer
on our knees than in the loftiest cathedral in the
world. Every temptation provides us an opportunity
to get closer to God. When the temptation comes,
don't look to the devil and to sin, look up to God.

IV. WE ARE TO LOOK UP TO GOD FOR COMFORT IN SORROW

This old world is filled with sorrow. When it comes
some people are beaten down into the dirt, while others
have the peace of God written in their faces. Although
troubles may come, let us learn that Jesus is the cure
for a broken heart. He said, "I will not leave you
comfortless. I will be with you always."

A certain woman went to church one morning. A
deep sorrow had filled her life, and she could find no
comfort. While she sat there in the pew a bird came
in at the open window, and flew up toward the ceiling.
The windows near the top were closed, and the poor
bird in seeking to get out to the open air again kept
flying against one window after another. In her heart
the woman was saying, "Why can't the poor thing
come down lower and see the open window there?"
Finally the bird grew weary and dropped to the floor.
As it did, it saw the open window, flew out and soon
was soaring away into the blue. Then the woman said
to herself, "I have been like that. I have been trying
to find peace in the wrong places, but Jesus has a

window open, and His arms are beckoning to me. I will humble myself and seek Him, and I shall find the light even as the bird found it." This woman found her comfort by simply yielding to Christ.

Look up, ye sorrowing ones, look up to the One who suffered for you on the cross. Say to Him, "O, thou who suffered more than any man, help me to suffer." And as you say that you will feel His arms around you and you will find your peace and comfort on His breast.

V. We Are to Look Up to God for a Vision of the World's Needs

Jesus said. "Lift up your eyes unto the fields, they are white already unto the harvest." As you lift your eyes you see the great needs and He comes to give you power to supply these needs and to help human hearts.

A certain man wanted to go to college and prepare himself for the ministry, but his health broke and he was greatly disappointed. With all hope gone he kept on crying, "I cannot be God's minister." But soon a voice came to him saying, "Go into business and give to it the same devotion that you would to the ministry. Make money and use it for God and His glory." The man arose with a new song in his heart. "I can be His minister—I can make money for Him," and he did make money and use it for the glory of God. He educated many others for the ministry and did a great work. You do not have to be a preacher.

God has a job for you right where you are. Look up and He will show you that task.

A missionary returned from the mission fields broken in health. One day as he thought of the needs of the foreign field, he said to the doctor, "I am not needed here, I am needed in China." But the doctor very wisely replied, "You are needed wherever you are." The truth went home to his heart. It is even so with all of us. God needs us wherever we are. He has a place of service for everyone of us.

VI. WE ARE TO LOOK UP TO GOD FOR POWER TO SERVE

What good does it do if we know the needs and are not prepared to help—if we do nothing about it? We need power for service.

Some years ago there was a barber in Italy who was said to be the greatest linguist in the world. He spoke four hundred different languages and dialects. The city gave him a pension so that he could continue his study. However, although he knew so many languages, he never rendered any service to anyone. What good does it do just to study and to have knowledge if you do not use your talents? You know the needs of the world, but what good is that if you are doing nothing to help the world?

Paul served God as no other man has served Him. He served Him in Asia and Europe and finally died serving Him in Rome. He established churches, won souls, wrote great books, performed many deeds. What was the secret of it all? He looked up to God. He

said, "I can do all things through Christ which strength-
eneth me." There are many tasks calling us. We cannot perform them ourselves, but we can with the help
of Jesus, if we simply remember to look up.

VII. We Are to Look Up to God for Future Provisions

Some day life will end for all of us. What about
the future? We can look up to God for that, for
Jesus said, "I am going to prepare a place for you."
He has provided a place big enough and grand enough
for us all.

In this world sorrow knocks at our door. We re-
fuse to open the door, but sorrow knocks down the
door and enters just the same. In life, trouble and
sin, tears and grief and death come to us and we are
forced to let them in. We have little power over them.
But when these things come to knock on the door of
heaven, God will say, "You cannot get in here." Nothing that hurts will ever enter into God's blessed Home.
Instead God has prepared a place where joy and
happiness and peace will reign forever more. If we
look up to God he will save us and make provision
for the long years of eternity.

After the battle of Inkerman during the Crimean
war, the stretcher bearers were gathering up the dead
and the wounded. They found the body of a young
man who had been fatally wounded, but who had
dragged himself into the shadows before he died. He
was lying with his head on his arms as if he were
asleep. As they reached his body they found an open

Bible beneath him. He had placed his bloody finger
on a certain verse and the congealed blood had caused
a portion of the leaf to adhere to the finger. As they
looked more closely they read the verse, "I am the
resurrection and the life ... He that believeth on me,
though he were dead, yet shall he live again." They
buried him with the text clinging to his finger. He
had died, but he had just begun to live. The struggle
of life was over, but the triumph of heaven had just
begun.

For all who trust Christ, for all who look up to
Him, God has provided better things than this world
can give. So let us say with the Psalmist, "I will
lift up mine eyes unto the hills from whence cometh
my help. My help cometh from the Lord."

4

CHRIST'S ANSWER TO LIFE'S HARD QUESTIONS

And behold, the half was not told me.—I KINGS 10:7

THERE IS located in Washington D. C., one of the greatest information bureaus in the world. People from all over the country send their questions to this bureau, the experts search out the information and then publish it in newspapers throughout the land. There are times, however, when even this great bureau is "stumped." They receive questions to which there seems to be no answer. In such cases, they appoint a special man to do research work and if there is an answer, he finds it.

But there are some questions which no human information bureau can answer. They are the deep questions of the heart and soul. No man on earth can answer them, but there is One who can. He is omnipotent, and omnipresent, and omniscient. Christ has the answers to all the hard questions of life.

Our text takes us to a palace in Jerusalem. The chief actors are two of the greatest rulers of the time. One is a man whose name is Solomon, and the other is a woman, the Queen of Sheba. She ruled over a

wonderful land. She was famous for her beauty and
power and wealth. She lived in a marble palace and
controlled millions of subjects. But there were questions in her heart that would not down. With all of
her wealth she could not find the answers for which
her heart longed. Then one day she heard of the
wealth and wisdom of Solomon. She heard more—
she heard that he knew about God. So she said,
"Maybe he can answer my questions. I will take the
long journey to see him." She then loaded her ser-
vants and camels with rich gifts, and after many days
finally arrived at the court of Solomon. The king
was very courteous. He showed her his palace and
all of the wealth and glory of his kingdom. They
then sat down and talked together for hours, and in
the conversation Solomon answered her questions about
God. Finally the queen felt that it was all so wonderful that she remarked, "The half was not told
me."

I do not know the questions which the Queen of
Sheba asked, but I do know this—you and I have
many hard questions in life, and the only place where
we can find the answers is in the heart of our King,
the Lord Jesus Christ. Let us make the journey to
Him today and ask Him certain questions.

I. What Kind of a Being Is God?

That is the first question—the universal question.
In the early days of the world Moses and others told
men about God. They knew that he was great and
high and holy and lifted up. David and many others

sang about the greatness of God; the prophets preached
about His judgment and love and mercy, but the people were not satisfied. He seemed still very far off,
and they wanted to see him. Their eyes were strained
for they had been looking up to God, whose face they
could not behold. It was only natural that they cried
out, "Show us the Father and it sufficeth us."

Suppose that in some foreign land there lived a
king who seemed to care greatly for you. He sent
you many gifts, gave you good advice and wrote you
many letters. One day a friend who had seen him
talked to you about him and praised him greatly.
Then you read a book about him. By that time you
would say, "I surely would like to see this king."
That would be a natural desire. So we do not blame
these men of old who said, "We would see God."

Jesus answered that question in person. He came
to the world and said, "Look at me and when you
have seen me you have seen the Father, for the Father
and I are one." Jesus is a perfect mirror of God.
When a man looks into His face he can say, "I have
seen God." Jesus, in coming down to earth, brought
God down to men and lifted men up to God. We
do not now think of God as a far off distant Being
who has no care for His children. We do not think
of Him any longer as a Giant sitting upon a throne
waiting for His children to sin that He might pounce
upon them. Jesus has brought Him very near. We
have learned to look upon Him as a loving Heavenly
Father, One who walks by our side and takes our hand
in His and who says, "Be not afraid, I am with you."

Would you know the character of God? Then look at Christ, who was holy and who had no sin in Him. Would you know the love of God? Then listen to this One who said, "Greater love hath no man than this, that a man lay down his life for his friend." Would you know the wisdom of God? Then listen to Jesus who "Spake as never man had spoken before." Solomon was the wisest of men, but we read that "A greater than Solomon is here." Would you know the sweetness and compassion of God? Then listen to Jesus as He says, "Come unto me all ye that labor and are heavy laden and I will give you rest."

On a very cold morning two men looked out upon a world encased in ice, with its beauty shining like diamonds in the sunlight. "It is beautiful, isn't it?" said the first man. "Yes," replied the other, "it is very beautiful, but it will all be gone before noon." "Never mind," replied the first man, "God will give us something else beautiful tomorrow." That is the kind of God He is. He is always giving us beautiful things. Jesus came into the world to reveal to us the kind of God He really is. Does your heart cry out for a knowledge of God? The answer is in Jesus Christ, His Son.

II. Second Great Question — What Shall I Do About My Sins?

This is the eternal question. Every man has had to face it, for every man has sinned. It becomes a load that we want to be rid of, a thorn that pricks

deeply. You may try every solution in the world, but
there is only one remedy, "The blood of Jesus Christ
cleanses us from all sin." The world has several answers to this question about sin.

(1) *Some say, "Deny the fact of sin."* They tell
us sin is only natural, that it is a human error, that
it is something in us for which we are not responsible.
But we know that sin does exist, for as we listen the
Bible cries out, "All we like sheep have gone astray."
"All have sinned and come short of the glory of God."
There is not a man upon the earth who has not sinned.
You and I do not know what other men have in
their hearts, but we do know our own hearts, and
every one of us must say, "I have sinned."

(2) *Some people try to cover sin.* One day God's
army in great power went up and took the city of
Jericho. God told them that they should not take
any of its wealth for themselves. A few days later
they went against the little city of Ai, and they failed
miserably. Why did they fail? It was because Achan
had stolen some of the forbidden treasures of the
city. They were found in his tent and he was sen-
tenced to death. He knew that he had sinned for he
said, "I saw—I coveted—I took—I hid." But you
cannot hide your sins. Achan learned this truth, "Be
sure your sins will find you out."

(3) *Some people place the blame of sin on someone else.* Adam, when he sinned, said, "The woman
thou gavest to be with me, she gave me of the tree."
But the woman said, "The serpent beguiled me." They
were simply "passing the buck" and men and women

have been doing this about sin ever since. The majority of prisoners in any prison will say to you, "I am here because of something that someone else did." Many a mother who seeks to excuse her wicked son says, "He was simply in the wrong company." Yet at the same time he is worse than any of his companions. No, we cannot place the blame for our sin on anyone else in the world.

Jesus has the only correct answer to the sin question. He doesn't tell you to deny it, nor to cover it up, nor to blame it on someone else. He says, "Repent of this sin, forsake it, confess it to God, bring it to me—I will take it and put it in the deepest sea where it will never bother you—where you will be safe from it forever more." Yes, you and I have sinned greatly, but "where sin did abound, grace doth much more abound."

A young Hindu said to a Christian missionary, "I have studied our two religions, and a Christian has one thing that Hinduism doesn't have." "What is the one thing?" asked the missionary. The Hindu answered, "A Saviour." There is the answer to the sin question. We have a Saviour who can really save us from our sin.

Our country has a huge deposit of gold in Fort Knox, Kentucky. This gold is surrounded by many tons of concrete and steel and a heavy guard is thrown about the fort every hour in the day. We say that this gold is safe. Yes, but not as safe as a Christian who has left his sin and come to Christ. He rests in the hand of Jesus; that mighty hand is closed over him. Then God's mightier hand is closed over this combination, and the soul is safe from the perils of sin forever.

III. What Is the Supreme Purpose of Life?

The why of life has always been a perplexing question. Many people have no real reason for life. Life is just one round of uselessness after the other. If you would know life's purpose, find it in the will of God, do it, and find a real joy in life. One follows the broad highway of pleasure and finds that its joys last but a season. Another goes out to make success— he gives all of life to that purpose, only to come at the end face to face with the eternal question, "What shall it profit a man if he gain the whole world and lose his own soul?" Another man tries to find the answer in worldly fame. He reaches the top, but finds that the paths of glory lead but to the grave.

There is only one place to find the true purpose of life. Go to the foot of the cross. What do you see there? It is a man dying, and you say, "I can learn nothing from him. He is thirty-three years of age, and is dying the death of a criminal. His life seems to be a failure to me." Ah me, from that figure on the cross we learn our greatest lesson. Here it is—the purpose of life is to give and not to get. "Except a corn of wheat fall into the ground and die, it abideth alone, but if it die, it bringeth forth much fruit."

The greatest souls in the world are the givers and not the getters. Who are some of the getters? Caesar,

Alexander, Nero and Napoleon. Who are some of the givers? Moses, David, Paul and Jesus. The first group lived their little lives and died and met death with the poorest of souls. The second group lived and served God and went out to meet Him unashamed. They learned that the true purpose of life was to serve God through serving others.

A business man once said, "My preacher is always talking about sacrifice. Frankly, I am tired of hearing it. There are other things to think about. I am afraid he is too visionary." Later this business man made a trip around the world, and his preacher said to him, "I want you to make a note of anything that you see which is unusual and tell me about it upon your return." Over in Korea one day the man saw a boy out in the field pulling a plow and an old man walking between the handles. The business man asked a missionary about this family, and he said, "We were building our little church sometime ago and this family was very eager to give something toward the construction, but they had no money. They did have an ox, so they sold the ox and gave the money to the church and now they themselves do the work of the ox." "But," said the business man, "wasn't that too great a sacrifice?" And the missionary replied, "They did not call it a sacrifice. They said they were glad they had the ox to give." When the business man reached home he told the preacher what he had seen, and then said, "I want to double my pledge and please give me some plowing to do. I am sorry that I never made a gift that cost me anything. That converted heathen taught me the real meaning of sacrifice."

Have you learned the real purpose of life? It is more blessed to give than to receive—not only with your money but with your whole life.

IV. THE LAST QUESTION — WHAT ABOUT THE FUTURE LIFE?

We knock at the door of all the philosophers and wise men, and they tell us that they do not know about the future life. But Jesus knows. He conquered death and rose from the grave. Out there in the vast unknown He stands saying, "I am alive forever more. Do not fear the hereafter. Trust me and one day you will be with me in the Father's house safe and comfortable and happy forever."

One day a woman came to Seneca, the great philosopher. She had had a crushing bereavement. He tried to console her, but he had no real message of comfort. He could only say, "Try to forget your sorrow. That is the only cure. Look at the birds — when they lose one of their number they fly away and promptly forget about it." What miserable comfort that was! There was no help in it at all. Yes, today we need to listen to One who can give us better comfort than that.

I am thinking of an incident that happened when I was just a boy. My father and I had been very far out into the country. It was mid-night when we reached home. The wind was blowing and the weather was hovering around the freezing point. My father went into the house and left me in the yard to un-hitch the horse from the buggy and take it to the barn. As my father opened the door to enter the house, I saw beyond that door the warm fire and the table where a good supper was waiting for us. Soon I put the horse away for the night, and started toward the house. Was I afraid to go in? No, because I knew that my father was waiting for me—that all was warmth and pleasantness inside and that the things which I enjoyed had been prepared for me. Some day our last little task on earth will be finished. Will we be afraid to go? No, for our Heavenly Father is on the other side of the door of death. He is waiting for us, and He is keeping for us all the joys and blessings of Heaven.

Jesus holds the answer to the question, "What about the future life?" He says, "Let not your heart be troubled. I am going to prepare a place for you." He is a great Saviour, my friend. He will answer all your questions and solve all your problems. Give your best to Him for this life and for the life that is to come. Do you know Him? Do you love Him? Are you serving Him?

> Sunset and evening star,
>   And one clear call for me!
> And may there be no moaning of the bar,
>   When I put out to sea,
>
> But such a tide as moving seems asleep,
>   Too full for sound or foam,
> When that which drew from out the boundless deep
>   Turns again home.

Twilight and evening bell,
  And after that the dark!
And may there be no sadness of farewell,
  When I embark;

For though from out our bourne of Time and Place,
  The flood may bear me far,
I hope to see my Pilot face to face
  When I have crossed the bar.
                        (Alfred Tennyson)

5

CHRIST'S SPOTLIGHT ON LIFE'S MYSTERIES

And the light shineth in darkness and the darkness comprehended it not.—JOHN 1:5

A GREAT SHIP was plowing its way homeward through the darkness. It was surrounded by such a dense fog that the pilot could see no more than a few feet in front of him. Suddenly his keen eye sighted the white foam of the breakers. He swung the ship about, but it was too late, and the vessel ran upon the rocks. The passengers and crew were rescued that night. In the morning when the fog cleared away they found that they were not far from a lighthouse. The lighthouse had been shining its beams out over the waves, but the fog was so dense that the light could not be seen by those on the ship. The light had been shining but the pilot comprehended it not.

A man in the far northwest was trudging home at midnight through a heavy snow storm. He was benumbed and cold, but he struggled on, hoping to get home safely. However, his strength finally gave out. He fell in the snow and froze to death. The next morning they found him in sight of home. The lamp had been burning faithfully in the window for him, but the darkness was so dense that he did not comprehend it.

Two thousand years ago Christ stood in the temple at Jerusalem. The great candelabra was lighted and the darkness in the temple disappeared. But He said, "I am the light of the world." His light was shining through the years of His ministry, but the darkness in human souls was so dark that they comprehended it not. "He came to His own, but His own received Him not." Through the centuries we have known of the Great Light, but there are thousands still who do not comprehend it. Every Sunday preachers stand and tell of the unsearchable riches of Christ. They are giving out the light, but thousands of people are going on in their sin and indifference. The Light is shining all right, but the darkness is so great that these souls do not comprehend it. O, that they might open their hearts and let the Light shine in their souls!

We have been in a dark building where we were unable to see anything about us. And then suddenly up near the ceiling a spotlight was turned on. Immediately a portion of the stage was illuminated and we saw clearly the people and the objects thereon. Jesus does just that. There are certain mysteries in this life which the great philosophers cannot explain. Only Christ can give us the light. In my previous sermon I spoke of the hard questions of life and how He answers these questions. Today there are five more questions that confront us. Let us ask Him to turn His light on these mysteries that we might know and understand.

I. Jesus Throws a Light on the Understand- ing of the Bible

The Bible is still the greatest book in the world. More copies are sold than any other book, more people read the Bible than any other book, more lives are changed and more hearts are touched by the Bible than by any other book. There are many who say, "I can- not understand the Bible." One reason they do not understand it is because they do not read it. But the Bible is not to be understood as other books. It is a spiritual thing, and spiritual things must be "spiritually discerned." If you do not know electricity, you can- not understand a book on electricity. If you do not know flowers, you cannot understand a book on botany. If you do not know Christ, you cannot fully under- stand the Bible.

Some years ago I was traveling along a lonely road at midnight. I had lost my way and I did not know whether or not this was the road that led to my des- tination. Then I came to a signboard which stood at the forks of the road. I turned my powerful head- lights upon this signboard. The directions were easily read and quickly I found my way home. The Bible is life's signboard, but we cannot understand it in the darkness of our own human wisdom. We must follow Christ and then as He turns the light of His spirit upon the Bible we see and understand.

Now the Old Testament is a great book, inspired of God and filled with wonder and majesty and beauty, but I say reverently that if the Bible ended with

Malachi, if we had no New Testament and no Christ, we could not fully understand the Old Testament, and we would have a confused idea of God. But Jesus throws light upon the Scriptures, and we know the kind of being God is and we understand the Old Testament because of Him.

There are three things that I wish you would do with the Bible. Learn it, love it and live it. You can read it as a mere book and it has nothing for you, but when you turn the light of Christ on it and let its truths sink into your soul, it will change your whole life. But what good will it do if we learn it by heart and do not live it? O, let us learn it, let us love it—but most of all, let us live it!

Jenny Lind was one of the greatest singers the world has ever known, but there came a time when she retired from the stage and from public life. A man came upon her one day sitting by the seashore, her Bible in her lap, and her eyes lifted to the sunset. He asked her why she gave up her stage career when all the world was at her feet. She replied, "I had to do it. Every day I was losing appreciation for that," and she pointed to the sunset. "And every day I was losing my love for this," and she lovingly laid her hand upon her Bible. It is true that if we give all of our lives to worldly things, the Bible loses its charm, but when we are living for Christ it becomes a new Book. Read the Bible and as you read it, pray that the Light of Christ may shine upon it.

II. JESUS THROWS A LIGHT ON THE MYSTERY OF PRAYER

A man in Europe speaks into a microphone and his voice travels over space and comes down into my living room. I cannot understand the mystery of radio, but I accept it just the same. Then I will accept this mystery also—that I, a little human being, just one of millions, can lift my heart to God and know that He hears and answers my prayer. There is no sound in all the world that pleases God more than the prayers of His children. His ears are always open and His heart is always listening.

Jesus helps us to understand prayer when he teaches us about the real nature of God, that He is a loving Heavenly Father. He said, "If a son will ask you for bread, will you give him a stone? If he ask you for fish, will you give him a serpent?" And then He tells us that if a human father, with all of his faults, answers the prayers of his children, how much more will our Heavenly Father answer the prayers of those who are His own.

In London a certain petition was circulated which was to be presented to the House of Lords. It was hoped that this petition would have great influence, but one little word was left out. Instead of saying, "We humbly beseech," the writers left out the word "humbly" and the petition was ruled out. So it is that if we want to make a appeal to God we must come humbly to His throne and He will not disappoint us.

A man had a little girl who was born deaf and dumb. He was devoted to her and gave all of his time outside of business hours to her. She loved him greatly, but could not express her love to him. Then there came a time when he had to go to Europe to spend a year. He put her in the best institution that he could find in America. During that year she learned to speak. When he came back from abroad and went to the institution, she rushed into his arms. She put her lips to his ears and said, "Daddy, I love you." He almost dropped in his tracks, because he did not know that she had learned to talk. He said these were the sweetest words that he had ever heard—the words of love that were spoken by his little girl. Somehow I think right there lies the beauty of all our prayers: just to tell God that we love Him greatly does wonders for us.

III. JESUS THROWS THE LIGHT ON THE MATTER OF OUR RELATIONS TO OTHERS

Life is a complex thing these days. It is a time of competition and friction. Every life is wrapped up in the lives of others. How can we keep these relations harmonious and helpful? Christ sums up the answer in the Golden Rule, "Whatsoever ye would that men should do to you, do ye even so to them."

What a wonderful world this would be if all of us followed that golden rule! Someone is treating you badly—lying about you, and hurting you. How should you treat them? Satan rises up and says, "Crush them, hurt them, get even with them." But Jesus says, "Do

unto them as you would have them do unto you." If
all of us would do this every bit of hatred and bitter-
ness in human life would soon die out.

President Harding once said in talking about inter-
national relations, "There has never been a better rule
than the Golden Rule." There never would be wars
in this old world if men and rulers would sit down
and say, "We are going to abide by just one rule—
the Golden Rule." That rule would simply settle everything.

Jesus gives us a lesson in neighborliness in the story
of the Good Samaritan. A poor man was robbed and
beaten and left half dead. Two representatives of religion saw him and passed by on the other side, but
one who was supposed to hate him had more compassion than the others. He bound up his wounds,
took him to an inn and paid his bill. Then we hear
the command from the lips of Jesus, "Go thou and
do likewise." When we bring this story down to prac-
tical everyday Christianity, what does it mean? It
simply means that regardless of whoever needs us, we
must reach down and help them out and help them
up.

The most wonderful people in the world are the
thoughtful people. That is what Jesus wants us to
be. It was said of Socrates "that he was all beautiful
within." Thoughtfulness of others is a mark of inner
beauty. Dr. H. M. Poteat, of Wake Forest College,
said that "a gentleman is distinguished from other in-
ferior types of men by his unfailing consideration of
the comfort and happiness of others."

IV. JESUS THROWS A LIGHT ON THE PROBLEM OF SUFFERING

There are many roses in the world, but it often seems that we have a dozen thorns for every rose. All of us are acquainted with trouble and sorrow. "Man is born to trouble as the sparks fly upward." But there is a Friend who can help us and will help us in this matter of human suffering. Is your heart troubled? Listen to Him as He says, "Let not your heart be troubled, ye believe in God, believe also in me." Just trust Him, for He was a man of sorrows and He knows what your sorrow is. Do you stand by an open grave? Remember that the tomb is dark no more, for He has put a light there. He said, "Because I live, ye shall live also." Is your heart torn by friends who proved false to you? He knows about that, too, for one denied Him and one betrayed Him. Have you felt that God Himself has departed from you? He felt that way, too, when He said, "My God, my God, why hast thou forsaken me?"

Summed up, I believe that the message of Jesus on suffering is this—"I know what suffering is. I have been through it all. When you suffer just trust Me. Keep close to Me and I will work it out for your good and the Father's glory." In the first World War our soldiers sang, "Pack Up Your Troubles in Your Old Kit Bag and Smile, Smile, Smile." We often wish that we could do that. We would like to pack them all up and throw them overboard. We cannot do that, but we can take them to Him and ask Him to help us with them.

After all, suffering is one of the best teachers that God has in the great school of life. Some of His greatest lessons are learned only at her feet. A young woman, who was suffering greatly, said to another woman who was a devout Christian, "If God loves me as you say He does, why did He make me so?" The older woman replied, "He has not made you— He is making you now." Suffering is often God's way of making us what we ought to be — what He wants us to be.

It is said that a bullfinch, before he learns to sing, must be placed in a dark room for many weeks. Then after he comes from this dark room into the sunlight, his song is sweeter and more beautiful than it could ever be otherwise. Often God must take us into the dark room of suffering in order to make us better, but when we come out again the song of life is sweeter and means more to the world than it ever would have otherwise.

V. Jesus Throws a Light on the Steps to Glory

Imagine a great flight of marble steps going up and up and up. At the bottom of these steps there are many people groping in the darkness for they cannot find the way out. But suddenly a great light shines upon these steps. All the people then see them clearly and with joy and singing they leave the darkness and climb the steps to glory. For many years we were in our sin; we groped about looking for a way out. And then Jesus came and He became the Light, showing us the steps that lead to Glory.

Some years ago, on Lincoln's birthday, a cartoonist drew a very effective picture. At the bottom of the picture he drew a log cabin. At the top of the picture he drew the White House. He then drew a ladder reaching from the log cabin to the White House and the title under the picture was this, "The Ladder is Still There." I would like to draw you another picture. At the bottom of that picture I would place the world with all of its sin and suffering and sorrow. At the top of the picture I would paint, if I could, a scene of the Heavenly Glory. And then I would place the cross of Jesus Christ as the steps that lead from this sinful world to that beautiful city. That ladder has been there throughout the centuries. It is there today and will still be there for all of those who wish to come His way.

There was once a man who was not able to see these steps. He went about the world blaspheming Christ, persecuting Christians and consenting to their death. But one day on the Damascus Road the Great Light shone about him and a Voice from heaven spoke to him. In this Light he found the steps to glory and years later when that man was nearing the end, he said, "I know whom I have believed and am persuaded that He is able to keep that which I have committed unto Him against that day. I have fought a good fight, I have finished the course, I have kept the faith; henceforth there is laid up for me a crown of righteousness, which the Lord, the righteous judge, shall give me at that day: and not to me only, but unto all them also that love His appearing."

Some years ago I was holding a meeting in my pastorate at Hendersonville, N.C. Night after night a man who was then seventy-six years of age would come to church. He listened attentively and his face showed that he was under deep conviction for his sin. Each night he would come to me and say, "Pray for me, I am a bad one." One night the Light shone for him. He was gloriously saved, and his sins were washed away. After that time he attended every service of the church and lived a faithful life for Christ. He died a little while ago at the age of eighty-two, but there was no sadness of farewell about his going. He had found the steps to glory.

My friend, Jesus can give you light for He is the Light. Yonder is a ship floundering in the stormy sea. The pilot sees a tiny light and steers toward it. As he comes closer and closer to the shore the light grows brighter, until it floods over the waves. He follows the light and soon is safe in the harbor. Jesus is the Light of the world. Have you caught a glimpse of Him? Then follow Him and serve Him. He will cause the light to shine about you. He will chart your course across the sea and take you safely home at last.

Many years ago a whaling ship was sailing through the South Seas in search of whales. One great whale was wounded and came charging against the flimsy hull of the little ship. A large hole was made in the vessel and the water came pouring in. Orders were shouted by the officers and soon all the boats were filled by the crew and by the necessities of life which they would require on the high seas. When they had gone a hundred yards out from the sinking ship, the boat stopped and two men suddenly jumped into the sea. They swam back to the ship, disappeared for a moment and then came back clutching in their hands the precious compass. They could not afford to leave it as they launched out upon an unknown sea. Listen, my friends, you are traveling the stormy seas of life. You must not leave Jesus out. He is our Compass—our Guide—our Light. Whatever your problem in life, whatever your sin, your trouble or your burden, just follow Him and all will be well forever more.

6

TWO SINNERS AT CHURCH

*Two men went up into the temple to pray; the one a
Pharisee and the other a publican.*—LUKE 18:10

The story of the Pharisee and the publican is the
story of two great sinners. One knew that he was a
sinner and acknowledged it before God. The other
knew not that he was a sinner and boasted of his
righteousness. It is a story of a good man who went
to hell and a bad man who went to heaven.

Yonder are these two men going to the temple.
One goes down to the front seat and proudly takes
his place there. He prays loudly, "Lord I thank thee
that I am not as other men. I do all these things
that are good and I do not do anything that is bad."
The other man felt so sinful and needy that he did
not even go into the temple. He stood afar off and
smote upon his breast and cried out unto God saying,
"Lord be merciful to me a sinner." Here we see two
different attitudes. One man is boasting of himself
and the other is pouring his heart out to God. One
man saw his great need, the other man saw his great
self. One man put himself on a pedestal, the other

man sank into the dust of humility and cried out for mercy.

We have these same two types of people today. We meet them on every side. One says, "I am a good man. Look at all the fine things I am doing. But look yonder at that person—what a shame. I am so glad that I am better than he is." The other man says, "Lord I am a sinner. I need help. I am guilty and I need mercy." He says nothing about anyone else. He just pours out his heart to God and tells Him about his own needs.

The time came when church was out and these two men went down to their homes. One walked pompously on his way, wrapped in his own importance and self-righteousness. The other went home thanking God—rejoicing that God had forgiven his sin and that peace was in his heart. And Jesus, the master story-teller, said, "One man went home justified, but the other one still had a sinful heart."

I. THE PHARISEE AT CHURCH

1. *He prayed with himself, not to God.* He was not praying to God, he was simply boasting to others and letting them know about the good things that he was doing. Jesus said, "The Pharisees love to stand praying in the market place that men might hear them." We have heard of preachers who would visit another church and go away angry because the pastor did not call on them for prayer. It is not the purpose of prayer to show off before men, but to pour out the heart to God.

When old Peter was sinking beneath the waves, he cried, "Lord save me!" It was a short prayer, but very effective. He did not pray for the benefit of the other disciples—he was not showing off—he needed help. The prayer of the Pharisee was not like the prayer of Peter.

A man dreamed that he went into a church just as the janitor was closing up. It was almost dark in the building. Up near the roof the man saw some birds fluttering about. They were trying to get out of the church, but could find no opening. He said to the janitor, "What are they?" The janitor replied, "They are some of the prayers which were offered here today. Only a few prayers get up to God. These will never reach Him, for they are mere words." The prayer of the Pharisee was like this and I am afraid that many of our prayers are also.

2. *He boasted of his morality.* He could say, "My life is clean. I have never stooped to immoral things." It is good to be able to say this. It is a pity that some cannot say it, and yet this alone will not save a man. Jesus said, "Blessed are the pure in heart, for they shall see God." We cannot see Him if we are not pure. There are many stars and mysteries of the universe which are hidden from the naked eye. They can be seen only through some great telescope. However, if there is a speck of dust on the lens of the telescope, the image is blurred. In order to see these stars the telescope must be kept polished. The soul is like that. Let impurities enter in and the sight of God slips away. It is only the pure eye that can see

God. May God help us in this age of loose morals
to keep ourselves pure and unspotted.

But there are many today who are building their
hopes of heaven on personal purity. They say, "My
speech is clean, I do not read rotten books, I do not
attend suggestive shows, nor walk the primrose path."
Personal purity is good, but if that is all you have
on which to base your hope of heaven, you are lost.

3. *He boasted of his business honesty.* He said,
"I do not cheat, I pay my bills, I am honest in all
of my dealings." There are many who drive hard
bargains to make a few dollars, they run up debts
which they cannot pay; they employ men and do not
give them a living wage. Men ought to be honest in
business, and yet honesty will not save a soul.

Why do not men take God into their business today? It is only rotten hypocrisy when a man's religion
makes him prominent in his church on Sunday and
does not influence him in his business each day during
the week. I know a good man who opens all of his
sales meetings with prayer. Why not? God is in-
terested in every phase of life and since our work
is such a big part of life, He ought to have a place
in it. And yet for a man to be honest is not enough.
That is a poor thing upon which to base your hope of
Heaven.

4. *He boasted of his religious life.* He prayed, read
the Bible, fasted and went to church, but these were
ceremonies with him and nothing more. These things
are not enough if the heart is not right. There are
many people who go through all these forms and yet

their hearts are black with hatred and enmity and jealousy and malice. If the spirit of Jesus Christ is not in every religious ceremony, that ceremony means nothing.

There are some who commit no sin of the flesh, but they are full of the sin of the disposition. They feel that they are all right since they never indulge in open sin, but at the same time they hate certain people, they are jealous and envious of others, they gossip and lie about others, and they try in every conceivable way to hurt them. Many repent of the sins of the flesh, but few feel any penitence about the sins of the disposition. They simply do not feel that they are sinners. Give me a man who says, "I am a sinner—God be merciful to me." Away with the man who says, "I am a good man, better than most of those I know."

We should never make a display of our religion. Recently I saw a young preacher walking down the streets of one of our cities. He had a big Bible under his arm, for he wanted everybody to know that he was a preacher. Another man whom I know would invariably come to church late, walk importantly down to the front and lay his Bible on the piano, as if to say, "I am a preacher, and I want all of you people to know what a good fellow I am." Let us not boast of our religion. Humility should be the first principle, the second principle, and the third principle of true Christianity.

5. *He boasted of his generosity.* He said, "I pay my tithe." How many of you are tithers? For your

own sake, the sake of your church, and the sake of the lost world and for Christianity's sake you ought to give at least a tenth of your income to God. But you say, "We are not under the law, but under grace." That is one big reason for tithing. God has blessed us more under grace than anyone was ever blessed under the law. "To whom much is given, much shall be required." The Jew under the law was in the twilight. We under grace are in the noontime of God's love.

Should we be stingy because God is good to us? Should we give less? God forbid—we ought to give more because of His kindness, but at least we ought to give a tenth. You will never be the Christian you ought to be until you learn to rightly relate your money to Christ. However, if you are trusting only in your generosity, you will be lost forever.

6. *He saw no flaws in himself.* He said, "I thank God that I am not as others." He divided society into two groups. He was in one group and everyone else in the world was in the other group. He was good and everyone else was bad.

I have heard someone say, "If everybody lived as I do this world would be a better place." They see the splinter in the eye of someone else, but never see the plank in their own eye. They are double-first cousins to the Pharisee. But you say, "You are not preaching to me. I do not need to repent. I am not a drunkard, I am not a great sinner." But I tell you that you do need a Saviour and unless you have Him you will be eternally doomed although you may have all these other things to your credit. "If we say we have no sin, we deceive ourselves, and the truth is not in us."

A man in a certain Scotch village owned a curious coat. On the front of the coat there were many large patches. He said that these patches represented the sins of his neighbors, and that every patch told of some sinful deed which they had committed. On the back of the coat there was a very small patch. When someone asked him what this patch represented, he said, "That is my own sin. I cannot see it." So it was with the Pharisee. He saw the flaws in others, but he could see none of his own. He has many relatives today.

7. *He despised others.* You may despise the criminal, and yet in God's sight you are no different. For we read in Romans 3:22-23, "There is no difference, for all have sinned and come short of the glory of God." Your love for God is measured by your love for men. If you despise others you do not have much love for the Lord.

William Borden had millions of dollars. He had every reason to be satisfied with a life of ease, but he loved Christ and because of that love he loved others. He worked in the slums of America and went abroad as a foreign missionary and died on the foreign field. Someone asked an English visitor to America what thing impressed him most, and he said, "The sight of this young millionaire kneeling in a mission station with his arm around a drunken bum, impressed me more than anything else in your country." Can you imagine the Pharisee doing that? No, and there are many others who would not do it. They are like this Pharisee—they have not Jesus in their hearts.

II. THE PHARISEE LEAVING CHURCH

He went away lost—He was not justified. Why?

1. *He trusted in himself.* He added up all the good that was in himself and trusted in that. Any man who does that is lost forever. There is only One Whom we can trust. We are to look away from self, look to the cross and trust Him only. Sometime ago a certain man died. He was not a Christian, but he was a prominent man and a good citizen. The minister at the funeral said, "I know this man went to heaven, for any world would welcome such a good citizen." That is not so—the Pharisee was a good citizen, but that was not enough.

2. *He did not acknowledge himself as a sinner.* Do you hear any confession in his prayer? There isn't a word of it there. A man never gets to God until he acknowledges his sin and feels his need of Him.

Dwight L. Moody said, "I can always tell when a man is a great way from God. That is when he is always talking about himself, how good he is." Proverbs 28:13—"He that covereth his sins shall not prosper; but whoso confesseth and forsaketh them shall have mercy."

3. *He did not cry to God for mercy.* He told God how good he was for he wanted God to admire him. He did not tell God how sinful he was and how much he needed God's mercy.

By nature we are sinners, and it is God's eternal law that sin shall not inherit the Kingdom of Heaven. He provides a way of escape for the lost soul, but this man was too proud to say that he was lost and needed mercy. My friend, you may not be a great sinner, but without Christ you are lost. You may be the best man in all the world, but without Him you have no hope. Wake up and cry to God for mercy! As long as you trust yourself and will not acknowledge your sin nor cry unto God for mercy, you are lost.

III. The Publican at Church

1. *He came to God humbly.* This man stood afar off. He boasted not of his goodness nor righteousness. A man must learn to kneel very low before he can enter the Kingdom of God. The Lord does not receive those who come to him in their own pride and self-importance. God received this man because he came humbly and in the right spirit.

2. *He came to God penitently.* He felt the weight of his sin. He was sorry for his sin and repented toward God for the sin. Why did he beat his breast? Because his sin was there—in his heart—and he wanted to be cleansed of that sin. That is what we need to do, to cry out, "Give me a clean heart, O Lord, take away my heart of stone and give me a heart of flesh."

I meet this man as he goes toward the temple. He has been scourged to the place of prayer by the deep need of his soul. I say to him, "I did not think you ever went to church." He replies, "I haven't been to church in years, but I am in trouble now and I must have help." He does not look around to see who is there. He does not talk about his own goodness. He does not think of the old hypocrite up there in the front row. He thought only of his own sin and his own need. To him there were only two persons in the world at this time—his needy self and a forgiving God.

3. *He came to God confessing his sin.* David cried out, "I have sinned." The prodigal cried out, "I have sinned." No man can get to Heaven until he has confessed his sin. There are some who will spend eternity in hell because they won't admit that they are sinners.

The people saw this publican as a careless, irreligious, Godless man. But one day there came a deep desire in his heart. He went to the temple and under the influence of these holy surroundings he felt himself a sinful man. No wonder he cried out to God. It would have been impossible for him to stifle the feeling that was in his heart. Today there are still many such as he. We may see no hope for them, but they are hungry for something that satisfies. We must do our part to bring the Gospel to them that they might be saved.

IV. THE PUBLICAN LEAVING CHURCH

1. *He left as a saved man.* Jesus said that he was "justified." That means that he was saved. Any man in the world who comes humbly as he did, who repents of his sin and confesses to God and cries for

mercy can and will be saved. But if you trust in your own goodness as did the Pharisee you will be lost forever. Why not throw all of your pride and self-righteousness away and fall at the feet of Jesus and be saved as was this Publican?

2. *He set an example for all sinners.* Can a sinner pray? Yes, here is his prayer—"God be merciful to me a sinner." After you have prayed this prayer and have come into right relationship with God, you are then ready to claim all of His other promises. If you will just pray this prayer tonight God will hear and will meet you half way to transform your life and to bless you forever.

In the military cemeteries of France the graves are marked by a simple cross. The women of France have volunteered to care for these graves. As a record of their willingness to assume this responsibility they write the two simple words, "I accept" on the cross, and then sign their names. I would have you look today to another cross. On that cross hangs the "very dying form" of the One who gave Himself for us. Won't you say today, "I accept; I take Him as my Saviour"? I beg you to follow the Publican and take his cry to your heart. Verily if you will do this you will go away from God's house justified and fit for heaven even as he was.

7

WHY I AM A CHRISTIAN

Men, brethren, and fathers, hear ye my defence which I make now unto you.—ACTS 22:1

Paul never lost an opportunity to tell how the Lord had saved him, the chief of sinners. He told his story before the rich and the poor, the great and the small, the high and the low, the king and the jailer. One day in Jerusalem the mob seized him and was about to kill him, but the chief captain rescued him and hurried him off to the castle. As Paul climbed the steps to the castle, he looked down upon that crowd of his persecutors and said to himself, "This won't do, I must speak to that great crowd and tell them about my Saviour." Turning to the captain he said, "Captain, may I say just a few words to these people?" The captain nodded consent, and Paul told them a great story for the glory of God. He told how he had kept the law, how he had persecuted Christians and consented to the death of Stephen. He told about his memorable trip to Damascus, about the light that shone on his path at noonday and the voice of Jesus speaking to him. He told about how he had been saved

and transformed, and as always he glorified God in
the telling of his experience.

Did you ever tell anyone how you came to Jesus?
It would do you good. It would refresh sweet memories
and draw you closer to the Lord. It would help others
and they would say, "If Christ did that for him, I
need Him also."

Why are you a Christian? Is it because your parents or your friends were Christians? Did you join the
church for business reasons? Then you are not a real
Christian. A real Christian is one who has had a vital
experience with the Lord. May I humbly tell you
several reasons why I am a Christian?

I. I Am a Christian Because in My Heart— As in Every Other Heart—There Is a Longing for a Higher Being

1. *This is a universal longing.* We find a longing
for God in hearts all over the world. When the man
in Africa worships the sun, he is expressing this longing for God. When the mother in India throws her
babe into the sacred river, she is expressing her longing to please a Higher Being. When an Indian talks
of the Happy Hunting Grounds, he is expressing his
longing for a superior One. The Greeks in Athens
worshipped "the unknown God," and this was simply
an expression of their longing.

There are some who say they do not believe in God,
and yet there are times when their hearts cry out for
someone greater than themselves. They may not call
that higher power God, but the longing is there just

the same. In our hearts and minds we long for a power that is greater than ourselves, a power that can lift us up and help us and comfort us.

2. *God alone satisfies that longing.*

(1) *Pleasure cannot satisfy.* You may go and indulge in all the pleasures of this world, but in the stillness of the night, when you sit alone with God, the fires of pleasure burned out, your heart still cries out for Him. I have tried it and you have tried it, and we know that the heart never finds peace in this world.

(2) *Money cannot satisfy this longing.* We have a mistaken idea that wealth will solve every problem. We say, "I would be happy if I just had plenty of money." However, those who have money know that it doesn't bring happiness. Some of the saddest people in the world are those who have money—and nothing else. Wealth cannot satisfy the soul nor the longing within it for God.

(3) *God alone really satisfies.* You may drink from all the wells of this world, but their water will not quench your thirst. But He says, "I am the water of life. The man who drinks of Me shall never thirst again." Some years ago I was holding a meeting in a certain church. On Thursday night of the meeting a young man came to me after church with tears in his eyes. He said, "I want to talk to you." We went to a quiet room and talked and prayed together. This man was gloriously saved in that hour. The next Thursday night he came back to me and said, "This

has been the best week that I have ever lived in my life—this one week that I have known Jesus Christ."

So I am a Christian because my heart cries out in longing for a Higher Being, and Jesus, the author of Christianity, satisfies that longing and fills the void in my aching heart.

II. I AM A CHRISTIAN BECAUSE I HAVE SINNED— AND WANT FORGIVENESS

All of us have sinned and when we come face to face with sin and all of its destructive power we cry out for forgiveness. When the eagle finds himself in a cage he wants to be free. He wasn't meant to be caged; he was meant for the higher heights. When a man finds himself bound in sin and feels the burden of that sin, he wants to be free, and because we have sinned and because He offers forgiveness we come to Jesus.

"There is now therefore no condemnation for them which are in Christ Jesus." My sin in God's book formed a record that was black and dark, but when we come to Him, His blood washes our sin away and at the judgment when He opens the big book He will say, "I have nothing against you." Thank God for a Saviour who can take our sins away.

Here is a convict who is in prison for life. But at Christmas time the governor comes and brings him a pardon and he goes free. The state can never try him on that same charge again. When we take Christ we have a pardon full and free and never again will be called on to pay for that sin. But there is a stain left on the convict's name. It is hard for him to get a job because of his disgrace. It is not so with the sinner. Christ even washes the stain away and the sinner is immediately taken into the Royal Family of God.

Once I was the prodigal son. I had gone far away from God and was spending my life in sinful living, but when I came home He took me in His arms; He put His best robe around me; He forgave me of my past and set me down at the banquet table of blessings and gave me the best that He had.

Yes, at the cross of Christ is the place to have your sins forgiven. How can you sit so complacently if you have never had this matchless experience? How can you eat and sleep knowing that your sin is carrying you to hell? Why do you wait? Yes, come to Jesus and you will know the sweetness of forgiveness.

III. I Am a Christian Because I Need an Outside Power in My Life Every Day

1. *I need a power to help me overcome temptations.* I cannot win alone. I often say, "I will," but I am doomed to failure when I trust in my own strength. I do not say that one who comes to Christ will never sin again, but I do say that He will give you strength to help you overcome temptation.

Jesus picked up a lily in His hand one day and said, "Behold the beauty of this flower. Even Solomon in all his glory was not arrayed like this." But did you ever see a lily growing in the black muck and mire of the lowlands? It doesn't stay in the mud, but lifts its head in all the purity and whiteness of this beautiful flower. We, too, are living in a world where we sink into the muck and mire of sin, but Christ will help us and give us power to lift ourselves out of this mud into the purity and whiteness of a beautiful life.

A man had fallen into the quicksand and was sinking down to death. A friend heard his cry and pulled him out. I was that man, and Jesus was that Friend. "I was sinking deep in sin" and I cried out unto Him for help. He heard my cry and pulled me out of the sinking sand. He is still that good, strong Friend. When I am tempted and call to Him He will lift me safely out.

2. *I need a power to bring strength and comfort to my life.* Often I feel like giving up. I say, "What's the use—everything is against me." And then Jesus whispers, "If God be for you, who can be against you?" Then I am stronger and better fitted to fight the battles of life. I cannot get along for one day without that outside power called God.

When sorrow comes, what shall I do? The preacher sees many breaking hearts. When those who grieve have no outside connection, they have no comfort. Bless God, I can say, "It is all well. All things work together for good to them that love God. Even this will come out all right." What would you do when your loved one slips away and your life is filled with sorrow if you did not have Jesus Christ as your Saviour?

IV. I Am a Christian Because I Appreciate God's Goodness to Me

1. *I appreciate His daily blessings.* Some people receive all the blessings of God and never look up to thank Him for them. The hog under the tree eats apples all day long and never looks up to see from whence they come. There are many people like that, but I want to be grateful to Him who carries me through each day and who watches over me each night.

I have made many dangerous trips in automobiles and planes and trains, but always there comes to mind this comforting scripture: "The angel of the Lord encampeth round about them that fear Him, to deliver them." Surely I would be a base ingrate if I did not appreciate the blessings that God sends to me from day to day.

2. *I appreciate the gift of His Son.* That is God's greatest and most wonderful gift. Many years ago France presented the Statue of Liberty to America. They were simply saying, "We are giving you this gift to show you how much we love you." When God gave His only Begotten Son to us he was simply saying, "I am showing you in this gift how much I love you."

A boy was captured by kidnapers and held captive for a long time. They demanded a great sum for his release. The father loved the boy so much that he gave a small fortune to get him back. We are captives of sin and God gave all that He had, even

His only Begotten Son, to redeem us from that sin.

I wonder if we appreciate the gift of His Son. We think of a man giving his blood to save a friend, and we say, "What a fine thing that is." But we sit silent when we know that Jesus Christ shed His blood for us. Surely out of our appreciation for that gift we ought to accept Him and live for Him.

V. I Am a Christian Because I Want to Be Ready for Death

I know not when that time shall come. I know not the day nor the hour, nor the year. I am not afraid, but if I were not a Christian I would be trembling with fear as I think of the future and of judgment and of eternity.

A little girl said to another, "I would be afraid to die." She later found Christ as her Saviour. The years went by and she was on her death bed. Her friend came to see her and said, "Are you afraid now?" With a smile she answered, "No, I am not afraid, Jesus has come for me."

Thomas Hobbes, the infidel, said, "I am taking a fearful leap into the dark." The Christian says, "I am not afraid, it is not dark, and He is holding me by the hand." On his death bed the Christian listens and hears His sweet voice saying, "Yea though you walk through the valley of the shadow of death, you may fear no evil, for I will be there with you."

When Dwight L. Moody was dying, he said, "Earth is receding, Heaven is descending, and I am going home." When Jesus is in your heart you are ready for life, for death and for the judgment. Are you ready?

VI. I Am a Christian Because I Want to Go to Heaven

I am not afraid of hell, but I want to go to heaven where I will see Jesus and all my loved ones and where I will live with them forever.

In one of our western cities there is a prominent institution at each end of the main street. At one end of the street there is a home for veterans, at the other end of the street there is a penitentiary for convicts. In a well ordered government we build a place for the good and a place for the bad. God has done the same thing. There are two ways of life. One ends in heaven and the other ends in the eternal night of hell. Which way are you going? The Bible tells us that hell is a terrible place. We read of "weeping and wailing and gnashing of teeth, and fire and brimstone and unutterable suffering." If we know Christ we need have no fear whatsoever, for He has locked the door to hell forever so far as His children are concerned.

I want to see Jesus and to thank Him for what He did for me. I want to see my loved ones, and put my arms around them once again in deepest affection. I want to find rest from all the troubles of this restless world. I want to live on forever in happiness and joy and I can do all of these things—because of Jesus and because I am a Christian.

An old sea captain, who lived in a home for retired sailors, was quite sick and near unto death. The chaplain of the home talked to him about Christ. He gave the old captain a Bible to read. He also gave him a red pencil and told him to mark the verses which helped him. One day the old captain's soul slipped away to be with God. The chaplain opened the captain's Bible and found that he had made a red circle around John 3:16. He had also made a little pasteboard anchor and left it at that place in his Bible. On the anchor he had written these words, "I have cast my anchor in a safe harbor."

Have you, my friend?

8

TOUCHED AND CHANGED

*And Jesus put forth His hand and touched him, saying,
I will; be thou clean. And immediately his leprosy was
cleansed.*—MATTHEW 8: 3

In one of our great cities a young mother with
her two-year old girl boarded a street car. Across the
aisle from them sat an old woman, grouchy, dirty
and repulsive. The little girl was just beginning to
talk. She soon became restless, and sliding down out
of her seat she walked over to the old woman and
put one hand upon her knee, and looking up into the
wrinkled face, she said, "I dot a Dranma at home.
I love Dranmas." The old woman was startled and
tears sprang to her eyes. She pushed the little child
away, saying, "I am not fit for you to touch me.
You are so pretty and sweet—go away." But the
little girl did not go away, she came even closer to
the old woman, and said again, "I love Dranmas."
The tears were soon overflowing the old face, and no
longer did the woman seem grouchy and repulsive.
All the passengers in the car saw the transformation
that had come to her. She had been made over in a
moment by a baby's tender touch.

90

But how much greater is the change when Christ touches one. A leper came to Him one day saying, "If thou wilt, thou canst make me clean." Jesus touched him and he went away whole and strong. A blind man came to Him—a man who had never looked upon the glories and beauties of the world. Jesus touched him and he went away, seeing all things. A crippled man came one day and Jesus touched the withered limb. The man was changed and went his way walking and leaping and praising God. An insane man out of the tombs came to Jesus. The Master touched him and he went his way a changed man, clothed and in his right mind. The widow of Nain wept as she followed her only son to the grave. Jesus touched him and the life flowed back into his body while the mother rejoiced over the fact that he had been "touched and changed."

But you say that miracles do not happen today. Yes, greater miracles than these are happening every day. Jesus said, "Greater things than I do, will ye do." The spiritual miracles that Jesus is working today through the Holy Spirit are greater than the physical miracles that came from His hands nineteen hundred years ago. Jesus still touches men and when He does the heart and life are wholly changed.

I. When You Are Touched and Changed You Have a Deeper Foundation

Watch them as they build a great skyscraper. Do they begin by laying the bricks and the stones on top of the ground? No, the first thing they do is to dig a yawning hole for the foundation. The steam shovel bites down deep into the earth preparing the way. Then the concrete is poured and steel is laid and a solid foundation is made. When a Christian life is built, the beginning is not made on the outside. No, you must go down deeper than that. The foundation must be laid in the Rock of Ages—Christ Jesus. If you do not build on that foundation your life will totter and fall. Time and tide affect concrete foundations, but nothing can shake the foundation of a Christian, for Jesus is that foundation.

Jesus told a story of two houses, one built upon the sinking sand and the other upon the solid rock. One house fell before the storm and the other stood staunch before every gale. Is your life founded on the sinking sands of this world, or is it founded on the Rock?

A world war chaplain was on board a ship in the Mediterranean. He stood on the deck talking to the captain, when suddenly there loomed up in front of him something that resembled a mountain. He asked the captain what is was and the captain said, "You have forgotten your geography. That is the Rock of Gibraltar." The chaplain thought of the civilization that had ebbed and flowed around that great rock. On the side of the rock he saw something that looked like a great white sheet. When he asked for an explanation, the captain replied, "Some years ago the British government found that the rock was crumbling on one side. They repaired it by putting this large slab of concrete right at the weakest point." Yes, time and tide leave their marks of decay on the historical old rock, but I know a rock that neither time nor tide can effect—it is the Rock of Ages, Christ Jesus my Lord.

> On Christ the solid rock I stand,
> All other ground is sinking sand.

Yes, when Jesus touches a life He lifts it out of the sinking sand, places our feet on the Rock and gives us an eternal foundation.

II. When You Are Touched and Changed the World Really Sees a Difference

In the slums of one of our cities there lived a man called "Old Born Drunk." As a baby his drunken parents had given him whiskey and he had grown to be a drunkard, the lowest of the low. But one day he heard the Gospel and the poor old soul wept his way to Christ. After his conversion he went into all of the old places distributing tracts and helping others to find the liberty that he had found in Christ. His life had been touched by Jesus and all men saw the difference.

When the world looked at the apostles of old we read, "They took note of them, that they had been with Jesus." That is the great trouble with our church members today. We cannot tell the difference between them and those who are in the world of sin. But we ought to see the difference. When a man has really been touched by Jesus there is a difference.

When winter comes we see the trees, bare and gaunt, outlined against the clear sky. But soon the spring is here and the whole world changes. We see the same trees green and heavy with leaves. They have been changed by the touch of spring. And so it is that when a life has been touched and changed by the power of Christ we find that that life bears the leaves of all the Christian graces. Yes, when Jesus touches one the whole world sees the change.

III. WHEN YOU ARE TOUCHED AND CHANGED YOU ARE MADE BETTER ON THE INSIDE

A young preacher tells of going out into the country to visit an old blind woman. As he approached her humble hut, he heard her singing an old-time hymn. He waited until the song was ended and then went into the house. The old lady talked about the goodness of the Lord, and finally the young preacher said, "Aunty, how long have you been a Christian?" She replied, "Nigh on to sixty years, and I ain't tired yit." She had something on the inside, something that was abiding and helpful.

The chief work of the Lord Jesus Christ is in the hearts of men. The world is not asking today whether you are a member of the church, or hold an office, or give to the church. They do want to know if Jesus is real to you, if He lives in your heart. If he has touched your life and changed it, you are made better on the inside.

IV. WHEN YOU ARE TOUCHED AND CHANGED YOU LIVE BETTER ON THE OUTSIDE

A little while ago I saw a group of workers putting up some power poles. Five or six of the men were handling the poles and the foreman stood some distance away directing the work. When the pole had been dropped into its hole the foreman wanted it lined up straight. He would give the signal and say, "Just a little more to the right," or "just a little more to the left." He wanted the pole to be straight and upright, for it was to carry the power to those who needed it. You and I as Christians are purveyors of spiritual power, and as such we must be straight and upright. If our lives during the week belie our profession on Sunday we have no influence for Christ.

When Lincoln's body was being carried through the streets of Albany, a negro woman said to her little baby, "Take a long look, honey, that is the man who died for you." I would take you to the cross and say to you, "Take a long look, man, woman, there is the Saviour who died for you." Realizing this, why can't we live better and let our lives shine for Him? I tell you that when Christ touches and changes a life, He not only cleans one up on the inside, but the outside is all different. God lives in it all the time, and other people feel the power of that good life.

V. WHEN YOU ARE TOUCHED AND CHANGED YOU HAVE A DIFFERENT SPIRIT

God said that Caleb "had another spirit." If we are touched and changed we have a different spirit. It is the Christian spirit. The spirit of Christ is the spirit of love and forgiveness, not for some, but for all. He loved those who loved Him, but He also loved those who hated Him. We often hear church members ᴛay, "I hate so-and-so. I would like to get even with him." Surely that is not the Christian spirit.

Jesus is the only one who has ever gone all the way in the matter of the spirit. Inside and outside He was perfect. His heart was pure and His spirit was right. Until we are living like Him we cannot say that all is well with our lives. There are many who think that if they never drink, steal or live immoral lives they are almost perfect. But simply to abstain from these things—to go to church and to give a little money is not enough. Unless you have the spirit of Christ in your everyday life, you have a long way yet to go.

Paul said, "If a man be overtaken in a fault, ye which are spiritual restore such an one in the spirit of meekness." Do modern Christians live by that rule? No, the tendency today is to kick the sinner farther down into the ditch of misery. This is not the spirit of Christ. If Jesus took that attitude there would be no hope for us in this world nor in the world to come. We can thank God that Jesus is loving and forgiving.

Do you want to get even with someone? That is not your business. God can handle the whole matter better than you can. Just leave it to Him, for He said, "Vengeance is mine, I will repay saith the Lord." Again He says, "If you forgive not men their trespasses, how can your Heavenly Father forgive you?"

If we have been touched and changed we should have this spirit. We love people, we forgive them, we help them all we can and simply leave everything in the hands of God.

VI. WHEN YOU ARE TOUCHED AND CHANGED YOU GIVE MORE

One of the laws of the Christian is that he is not always seeking to take in everything for himself. He is often giving out to God and to others. He gives his time, his talents and his money to this old needy world. When Jesus touches him he says, "These things are not my own. They are His and I will give them to the world for His sake."

I spoke sometime ago on "Crowds of Souls." That is the way the Christian should look upon people. They are souls, hungry souls, needy souls, lost souls, eternity-bound souls. Christ counts on the Christian to win them and to help them. When He looked upon a crowd three things happened. He saw human beings, His heart went out to them, and He helped them. If you belong to Him you will do likewise. You will see the world and have compassion on it and then do something about it.

Giving does something for people. It makes them more considerate of others. The trouble makers in most churches are those who give the least. The consecrated members are those who love God and love others. They have been touched and changed, and they always give out more after that experience with Jesus, the Great Giver.

VII. WHEN YOU ARE TOUCHED AND CHANGED YOU HAVE A BETTER FUTURE AWAITING

There is where the great difference comes in. It often happens that a Christian has a harder time here than the non-Christian. But out yonder in the future the Christian has a hope, while the other man has none. This is all that will count at the end of the way. It will not matter then how much money you have made nor how much pleasure, fame and power have been yours. The only thing that will matter will be this, "Do you have a hope in Christ for the future?"

Here is a train running along on a side-track, but the switch-man throws the switch and the train soon runs onto the main line and comes safely to the station at last. You and I have been running on the side-track that leads to hell, but when we are touched by Jesus the route is changed. We get on the main line of salvation and we enter the heavenly station at last.

An old soldier had lived through many adventures, thrills and experiences. He was telling a group of tourists about his life one day, and they were amazed at the marvelous drama of that life. And then he shocked them by saying, "I expect to see even greater surprises yet than I have ever known." They said to him, "You are an old man. How do you expect to ever have any adventure to surpass these you have told us?" And the old man humbly replied, "I will know the greatest thrill of all in the first five minutes which I spend in heaven with my Lord."

Thank God for the touch of Jesus! Thank God for the change that He makes in us! Where would we have been if he had not come? Since He has done so much for us, we ought to give our lives in full surrender to Him. May God help us to be faithful to the Lord Jesus Christ.